CARLSBAD CAVERNS

BY
Lewann Sotnak

I wish to thank John Roth, Park Ranger at Carlsbad Caverns National Park, for his help in researching this book.

PUBLISHED BY
CRESTWOOD HOUSE
Mankato, MN, U.S.A.

LIBRARY OF CONGRESS CATALOGING IN PUBLICATION DATA

Sotnak, Lewann.
    Carlsbad Caverns

(National parks)
Includes index.
SUMMARY: Describes the formations of plant and animal life of Carlsbad Caverns and examines the history of the national park which they have become.
    1. Natural history — New Mexico — Carlsbad Caverns National Park — Juvenile literature. 2. Carlsbad Caverns National Park (N.M.) — Juvenile literature. [1. Natural history — New Mexico — Carlsbad Caverns National Park. 2. Carlsbad Caverns National Park (N.M.) 3. National parks and reserves.] I. Title. II. Series: National parks (Mankato, Minn.)
QH105.N6S68   1988   508.789'42—dc19   88-17707
ISBN 0-89686-403-0

International Standard Book Number:	Library of Congress Catalog Card Number:
0-89686-403-0	88-17707

PHOTO CREDITS

Cover: Journalism Services: Dave Brown
Animals, Animals: (Stephen Dalton) 25; (Roger Jackman) 43
DRK Photo: (Marty Cordano) 29; (Stephen J. Krasemann) 30-31, 32; (C. Allan Morgan) 34; (Pat O'Hara) 39
Journalism Services: (Dave Brown) 4, 8, 10, 12, 13, 16, 20, 22-23
Tom Stack & Associates: (Robert C. Simpson) 7; (Richard P. Smith) 11; (Dick George) 14-15, 41; (Ann & Myron Sutton) 18-19; (Ann Duncan) 21; (Jeff Foott) 26; (John Gerlach) 36

Copyright © 1988 by Crestwood House, Inc. All rights reserved. No part of this book may be reproduced in any form without written permission from the publisher, except for brief passages included in a review. Printed in the United States of America.

Produced by Carnival Enterprises.

Box 3427, Mankato, MN, U.S.A. 56002

TABLE OF CONTENTS

The Amazing Discovery...5
The Caverns Become A National Park...6
Inside The Caverns..7
Scenic Rooms...11
Big Room...15
How It All Began...17
Bat Flights...24
Bat Guano Mining...25
The Chihuahuan Desert...27
The Guadalupe Mountains...33
Animals Of The Area...34
New Cave..37
Early People Of The Region...38
Taking Care In The Park..39
Accommodations In The Caverns...40
Area Information..42
Activities Above Ground..42
For More Park Information...44
Park Map...45
Glossary/Index...46-47

Visitors who explore Carlsbad Caverns see beautiful formations.

Carlsbad Caverns National Park

THE AMAZING DISCOVERY

It was the year 1901. A 19-year-old cowboy named Jim White was riding his horse in the Carlsbad area of New Mexico. Suddenly he saw a black cloud rising from the earth and spreading out in the sky like a funnel. Was it smoke, or was it a volcano coming to life?

Jim urged his horse up a steep cliff. When he was closer, he saw that the cloud was really millions of bats pouring out of the mountain. Jim tied his horse and climbed the rest of the way on foot.

The powerful odor of bats would have turned back a person with a weaker stomach. But Jim knew that any place that held this many bats had to be very big, and he wanted to see it. When he reached the spot, he lay down at the edge of the cliff and peered over. Below him yawned a huge hole in the mountain. It reminded him of a whale's open mouth. "How far down inside the earth does that hole go?" Jim asked himself.

The next day Jim came back with some rope and a kerosene lantern. First he built himself a ladder using the rope and some strong sticks he had cut. Then he climbed down into the inky blackness. Part way down he reached the end of his ladder, but he was in luck. His feet touched a ledge. Here he tied another rope to the last rung, and with his lantern he struggled down to the floor of the dark, silent cave.

5

As Jim walked back into the caverns, he was astonished at what he saw. There seemed to be miles of passageways and rooms that branched off into new ones. Jim soon realized that he could be lost forever if he wasn't careful. He grabbed handfuls of pointed rocks and laid them out like arrows to mark his way back to the entrance of the cave.

Jim continued exploring, far into the caverns. Strange shapes and magnificent formations appeared to be chiseled in stone. It looked like a master sculptor had been at work. The stone shapes looked like animals, people, flowers, and birds. Some resembled chandeliers, pillars, domes, folds of draperies, castles, and statues. Stone icicles hung from the ceiling. Great shapes grew up from the ground.

From this day on, Jim's life was changed. He spent the rest of his life exploring the caverns, guiding others through them, and trying to interest the outside world in his magnificent discovery.

THE CAVERNS BECOME A NATIONAL PARK

Many discouraging years went by before anyone would even listen to Jim's story of what he had discovered in the caverns. People laughed at him and called him "Bat Man" and a liar. Others said it wasn't possible for there to be caverns as he described. If Jim had been able to take pictures, people may have believed him sooner. But at that time, flash cameras were not common. Those who did have expensive flash powder equipment wanted too much money for taking the pictures.

"Just wait," Jim told the disbelievers. "Some day people will come from all over the country to see these caverns."

Over the years, reports of these fantastic caverns were heard around the country. People began to visit, and they told others. Important government officials came. Jim took them on tours through the cave. They discovered that Jim was not lying after all. This was something to see!

Finally, in 1924, the National Geographic Society became interested, and Jim guided one of their parties through the caverns. In 1930, the Carlsbad Caverns were declared a national park. Jim's 29 years of stubborn patience had paid off.

The main entrance invites visitors to the amazing underground world of Carlsbad Caverns.

INSIDE THE CAVERNS

The caverns are very deep. They go as far down into the earth as the Empire State Building in New York City goes up into the sky!

Those who enjoy hiking can take the long walk down the *switchback* trail to the natural entrance of the cave. Others may catch a quick ride on elevators directly to the bottom of the cave.

After visitors enter the caverns, they pass the gloomy, unlit passageway that leads to Bat Cave. No one stops to visit the bats!

Beyond Bat Cave, tourists begin to see some of the amazing formations that Jim White saw with his kerosene lantern. Now electric lights make these formations easy to see.

The stone icicles you can see throughout the cavern are called *stalactites*.

FUN FACT At one time there may have been as many as 12 million bats living in Bat Cave during the summer.

Stalactites can be as thin as straws or as thick as a baseball bat.

They hang from ceilings, walls, and ledges. The icicles usually have sharp points, and many are as tiny as soda straws. Sometimes stalactites grow together in sheets that look like curtains or draperies. Others may have a covering of bumpy crystals that look like popcorn.

Stalagmites grow up from the ground. Their tops are usually rounded. Some stalagmites are small. Others can be as big around as water tanks, or as tall as six-story buildings.

Here's a good way to remember the difference between stalactites and stalagmites: Stala*c*tite has a *c* in it and hangs from the *c*eiling. Stala*g*mite has a *g* in it and *g*rows up from the *g*round.

Many stalactites and stalagmites have grown toward each other until they touched. They have became columns.

Helictites are another wonder. They look like plants with crystal branches that twist and turn in every direction.

Visitors will also see *flowstone*, a colorful coating of minerals on floors and walls. There are stone *lily pads* made up of minerals that have formed on top of cavern pools. Shiny, round *cave pearls* lie in shallow pools that resemble stone nests. The pearls were formed when lime grew around single particles of sand. As water dripped slowly into a pool, these particles turned round and round. Layer upon layer of mineral was added until cave pearls grew to the size of real pearls. Others became as big as golf balls.

In Carlsbad, a visitor's adventure begins in the Main Corridor. This is a long hall with a 200-foot-high ceiling that reminds many people of a cathedral.

The trail through this corridor goes down and down, a descent of more than 800 feet to the caverns below. Along the way are interesting formations. There is Devil's Spring, where dripping water has formed a small pool. Whale's Mouth is wide open, showing off a ridge of fringed flowstone. Visitors walk through Devil's Den or across Natural Bridge. Next is American Eagle with a wing spread of 12 feet. Witches Finger is a stalagmite that points with a long, narrow, crooked finger. Baby Hippo is here, too, and Three Little Monkeys sit high above the trail.

At the end of the long hall sits The Iceberg. This huge heap of stone weighs more than 200,000 tons. It fell from the cave's ceiling thousands of years ago.

FUN FACT Dripping stalactites and stalagmites grow so slowly that it takes about 85 years for them to develop one new coating of minerals. This layer is only as thick as a coat of paint.

The Veiled Statue stalagmite "grows" up from the ground.

SCENIC ROOMS

After leaving the Main Corridor, visitors can see the Scenic Rooms and other interesting formations along the way. In silent stone stands Veiled Statue, formed when a stalactite met a stalagmite. Frozen Waterfall and Bashful Elephant, with its back side toward visitors, are two more formations nearby.

"Lion's Tail" is found in one of the deep rooms in the cavern.

The Green Lake Room is decorated with hundreds of formations and an eight-foot-deep lake.

Green Lake Room looks like a wonderland. Thousands of stalactites hang from the ceiling. Flowstone, looking like marble, decorates the room. A greenish lake, eight feet deep, gives the room its name.

In King's Palace, countless icy stalactites glitter like chandeliers. This room looks like an emperor's ballroom. With imagination, one can almost see the emperor raise his hand, giving the signal for the ball to begin. The King's Bellcord hangs here, too. It is a stalactite that is seven feet long and as slender as yarn.

FUN FACT The temperature in the caverns never changes from 56°F. That's because the earth is so well insulated by all the rock that it holds the temperature at a constant level.

Around every turn, visitors can see formations of flowstone, stalagmites, and stalactites.

Nearby is the Queen's Chamber. Its floor and throne are covered with graceful flowstone. Masses of stalactites have grown together to form silken draperies. No queen is present, but the King's Boots hang in her chamber.

A small room called Papoose Room shimmers with slender stalactites. They stick out from the low ceiling like porcupine quills.

The Guadalupe Room is a more recent discovery. It is the second largest room in the Carlsbad Caverns, but it is not open to the public. Getting inside is too difficult. First, you have to crawl along a narrow passageway. At one

Visitors to Mirror Lake can find out its name by reading the sign's reflection in the water.

point the passage is shaped like a U. Here, you must pull yourself through the loop. It is no place for those who are afraid of tight squeezes!

After a steep drop down an incline to the floor of this huge room, there are beautiful things to see. You can see dripping water everywhere. There are thousands—maybe millions—of stalactites. Waterfalls look as if they were frozen in stone. Graceful stalagmites stand guard. Brilliant yellows and oranges decorate the room. There is a small, yellow, stone canary, perched with its head raised. Those with imagination might hear it sing!

FUN FACT The deepest chamber in the Carlsbad Caverns is more than 1,000 feet below the surface.

BIG ROOM

As far as anyone knows, Big Room is the largest underground chamber in the world. In places the ceiling is more than 220 feet high! This room could hold 14 football fields. The United States Capitol Building would fit in one corner. Because of the twisting trail, it's hard for people to tell that it's all one room.

The walls are hung with stone draperies. Stalagmites grow up from the floor. Stalactites, like ribbons and soda straws, are everywhere. Frozen waterfalls look as if they had turned to stone in mid-air.

> FUN FACT The Bifrost Room is a recent discovery in the caverns. Its beautiful formations are so fragile that, at first, only cave specialists were allowed in the room in their bare feet. Now, no one may enter. Fortunately, pictures have been taken of the place. To reach the room, one must climb up a 60-foot wall.

Millions of years ago, the area where Carlsbad was formed used to be only a shallow sea.

Within this room there is the Hall of Giants, where domes of stone stand guard. One of these giants is nearly 60 feet high.

Temple of the Sun has never been touched by the sun's rays, but electricity lights up its thousands of stalactites. These shining icicles make the ceiling look like an upside-down pin cushion. The Big Room trail passes Bottomless Pit. Early explorers thought this pit had no end. Now its floor can be seen with a flashlight. Only those who work for the park may swing down to the bottom on a rope. Santa Claus, Statue of Liberty, Totem Pole, and the famous Rock of Ages are other formations seen in this amazing room.

Another place visitors may not go is Lower Cave. As far as anyone knows, it is the deepest part of the caverns. To get to Lower Cave, park employees use a rope at Jumping Off Place and swing down to the bottom.

Here lies a beautiful clear lake, gleaming in the lamplight. It is called Lake of the Clouds because the shapes above look like towering thunderheads. The water is always fresh because it has no living matter in it to rot or decay. Rain water filters down through many layers of earth and rock before it drips cool and clean into the Lake of the Clouds.

HOW IT ALL BEGAN

About 255 million years ago, the area where the Carlsbad Caverns began was only a shallow sea. A rocky ridge or shelf called a reef grew by the shore. This U-shaped reef was several hundred miles long. *Algae* and tiny sea creatures lived on the reef. As the algae and tiny creatures died, they mixed with the remains of other animals like clams, sponges, and snails. Combined with sand, shells, and pieces of rock, they built the reef bit by bit, higher and higher. As the reef grew out into the deep sea, it cracked in many places. Eventually, the ocean dried up and the reef was covered with sand and soil.

Much later, the dinosaurs were dying out. Powerful forces began to work inside the earth. They pushed up rock to make mountains. These forces also pushed, pulled, and squeezed the *limestone* reef until it developed larger cracks. Water in the ground and from rain and melting snow flowed into these cracks.

A weak acid in the water called *carbonic acid* dissolved the soft limestone in the rocky cracks. This hollowed out cavities and caves, much as the fizzy carbonic acid in soda pop hollows out little caves or cavities in people's

FUN FACT In Big Room there is a stalactite and a stalagmite that grew towards each other over thousands of years but never touched. Because they are only a knife's blade away from each other, they are named Frustrated Lovers.

Lights shine on Temple of the Sun to create a wonderful sight.

Skinny "soda straws" are the beginnings of stalactites.

teeth.

    The earth pushed the limestone reef up and up to form the Guadalupe Mountains. As the mountains rose, the water drained from the caves and caverns. Air filled the chambers. But ground water and water from snow and rain seeped into these caverns. The water, which was full of dissolved minerals, dripped from the cave's ceiling. Every drop left behind a tiny mineral deposit shaped like a ring. As the rings built up they formed small tubes. These tubes grew longer into forms called soda straws. When the straws became blocked, water trickled down the outside. This caused the

FUN FACT Carlsbad Caverns is one of more than 70 known caves in the Carlsbad Caverns National Park area.

tubes to grow fatter until they formed stalactites.

Water also dripped onto the floor. The water deposited minerals too, but this time on the floor. The deposits got higher and higher until they "grew" into stalagmites. It took the water drops hundreds of thousands of years to grow into all the amazing formations that are seen in the caverns today.

Water dripping onto the cavern floor deposited minerals that built up higher and higher to form stalagmites.

A cavern with all its beautiful formations takes thousands of years to develop.

BAT FLIGHTS

There is no way to hide millions of bats. Long before the caverns were ever explored, people saw the bats flying out of the cave every night. In those early days it took as long as four hours to empty all those bats from their home!

Native Americans and early ranchers knew about the cave because of the bats. But people were not interested in exploring such a place. They never dreamed there were so many miles of corridors and rooms filled with fantastic formations. They only knew that there were bats in that dark, smelly cave. And for all they knew, a few spirits might be lurking there, too.

The number of bats today is much less than it once was. Instead of millions, there may be 100,000 or more (which is still a lot of bats for one cave). There are fewer bats in Carlsbad because of poisons that have been used to destroy insects. As the insect population has grown smaller, so has the number of bats, who depend upon insects for food.

All night long the bats swoop and dive as they hunt. They stuff their stomachs with moths and other insects that fly at night. Bats may hunt as long as ten hours and fly as many as 150 miles. Because they hunt in total darkness, they depend on a *sonar system*. They give off sounds that are too high-pitched for human ears to hear. The echoes from these sounds bounce off objects. This keeps the bats from bumping into things. It also helps them find food. At dawn the bats fly back into the caves where they hang upside down, clinging to the ceiling.

A bat is not a bird. It is a mammal. That means that its babies are born alive instead of from eggs. Mammals also drink milk from their mothers. As soon as the babies are born, they cling to the ceiling or to their mothers while they nurse. In the evening, the mother goes off as usual to hunt insects. When she returns to the cave, she is not fussy about finding her own baby. She settles next to any one of them that will nurse from her.

When the baby bat is big enough to fly, it lets go of the ceiling and takes off to hunt. If for some reason it can't fly, it falls to the cave floor and dies. The most common bat found in the Carlsbad Caverns is the Mexican free-tail bat.

Visitors to Carlsbad Caverns may gather near the entrance in the evening to watch the bats take off for the night. Before the flight begins, a ranger gives a short talk. Suddenly, perhaps awakened by an inner clock, the bats begin

FUN FACT The bats from Carlsbad Caverns may eat as much as a ton of insects in one night.

to spiral from the cave. They make a huge cloud, just like the one Jim White saw so many years before.

Tourists who are willing to get up at dawn can watch the bats return. A "bat flight breakfast" is planned once a year in August by the people who work for the park. Visitors have ringside seats. Here they can watch as the bats sky-dive back to the entrance and zoom into their sleeping quarters.

In the autumn, the bats migrate to Mexico for the winter.

BAT GUANO MINING

There is another story about Jim White. One day, when he was working on the ranch, a man came to see him. "My name is Abijah Long," said the

The hundreds of bats that live in parts of the caverns leave at dusk to find food.

man. "I'm interested in your cave."

Jim shook with excitement. "I'll take you there! Why, you've never seen such formations. There are..."

"Hold it!" said Abijah. "I'm only interested in bat guano."

"Don't you want to see the rest of the caverns?" asked Jim.

"Not unless they have guano in them," replied Abijah Long.

Bat guano is another name for bat droppings. For thousands of years, millions of bats had slept in that cave. As they clung to the ceiling, the bat droppings piled up. Deeper and deeper grew the layers until the guano was higher than a tall house.

When Abijah saw the guano, he shouted for joy. "Must be a hundred feet

Bats depend on their sonar system to guide them around in the dark.

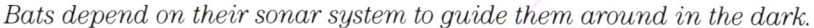

of guano in here! Those California fruit growers will pay a good price for this." Fruit growers all over the west needed fertilizer for their crops. Bat guano was just the thing.

After Abijah worked out his plans for the mining operation, he hired Jim to supervise the project. Supervising was a very big job. Food for the workers had to be hauled in by mule 26 miles each day. Then it was lowered into the main cavern to keep it cool. Wood and dead shrubs needed to be gathered for the cooking fires. A little burro named Joe walked a mile to a spring with Jim several times each day. They brought back gallon cans of water strapped to Joe's back.

Each day the men were let down two at a time in a big iron bucket tied to a rope. Then the miners shoveled the guano into gunny sacks. They hoisted it back up in the same bucket.

Jim had to keep hiring new men all the time. Some quit because they couldn't stand the powerful smell of the bats. Others were afraid of the dark, the shadows on the walls, or the sleeping bats above them.

Jim tried to interest the miners in seeing the rest of the caves. But most of them were too tired after a hard day's work. Some were afraid of the dangers in the caverns. Others worried that something might be hiding in the dark passageways.

Ten years after he began supervising the mining operation, Jim White got married. The mining company built a small house by the caverns for him and his wife. Soon a son was born; eventually the mine closed down. Jim, his wife Fannie, and their son continued to live in their little house. Jim was relieved that the mining had ended. He went on exploring the caverns and discovering new things.

Before long, visitors were coming from all around to see the caves. Fannie helped out by cooking hearty meals for the explorers to eat after they came out of the caverns with Jim.

THE CHIHUAHUAN DESERT

Above the Carlsbad Caverns and within the boundries of the national park lies the Chihuahuan Desert. The whole desert stretches across part of New Mexico, Texas, and on into Mexico.

At first glance the desert may look bleak and bare. But there are many

FUN FACT In the caverns there is a bat that has become part of a stalagmite. It might have died when it got lost a long time ago. Water dripped over it for thousands of years as the stalagmite formed. Today visitors can see the outline of its wings and head.

kinds of plants growing in the dry, dusty soil. Learning the names of these plants can be confusing. People living in different places may have given different names to the same plant. Some plants have as many as seven different names.

A cowhand once said that everything on the desert either sticks, stinks, or stings. These are some ways that desert plants protect themselves and save water. Since rain may fall only once a year, or even less, the plants can't waste a drop.

Trees lose a lot of water through their leaves, so desert plants do not have leaves like trees. Instead, some have barrels. The barrel has a fluted edge, so it can stretch to hold more water when the rains come. In dry times it shrinks.

One plant is called David's walking stick. Most of the year it looks like a plain old stick, standing straight up in the ground. When it rains, this old stick looks as if it has been touched by a magic wand. Long, red, spike-shaped flowers appear. Birds and insects fly in to feed on nectar in the flowers.

The prickly pear has flat, oval pads covered with thorns. During the rains, yellow or orange rose-like blossoms come out. Later in the summer, the deep green pads are covered with fruit called tunas. Tunas are the size of figs and are filled with reddish juice. Animals and people like the taste of them. A wild goat munching on tunas is quite a sight with red juice running down its neck and onto its chest. Goats are not fussy eaters. They will gobble up the thorns and all.

Broomweed and agave are two other plants common to the desert. Agave was a popular food with Native Americans.

Yucca, a very tall plant, is the state flower of New Mexico. There are many kinds of yucca. The Native Americans used it for making rope, mats, sandals, and baskets. Its sharp, thorny leaves provided paint brushes and needles. Some Native Americans still use the plant's roots for making soap and shampoo.

Sotol is another desert plant. Near some cities this plant was in danger of dying out. That's because people picked and sold them for "desert spoon" souvenirs. Now these plants are protected by law.

Although there are no pet cats living on the desert, there are plenty of cat's claws. Cat's claw is a plant that has short, curved thorns that look like the claws of a cat. Hikers and bikers hate these plants because the claws tear

Above ground, the desert around Carlsbad Caverns is home to many colorful plants.

After it rains, yellow or orange petals bloom on the prickly pear.

their clothes and scratch their arms and legs. The Native Americans ground the claw seeds into meal and used it for cooking.

Greasewood, named by Native Americans, is a plant more commonly named creosote. The creosote plant is full of something called resin. Resin is like an oil that coats the leaves. This keeps out the desert sun and holds moisture inside the plant. Animals leave this plant alone because it tastes terrible!

There is an old legend about greasewood. Long ago there was nothing, only darkness. Then a spirit grew inside the darkness, and the spirit became Earth Maker. Earth Maker took a handful of soil from his body. He shaped and molded this mound of earth, and the first thing that grew from it was the greasewood.

THE GUADALUPE MOUNTAINS

In the middle of the Chihuahuan Desert rise the Guadalupe Mountains. They stretch out mile after mile through part of New Mexico and into Texas. They are rugged, beautiful mountains, dented with scenic canyons.

On the slopes a variety of bushes and trees provide food and homes for wild animals. Pine, firs, and aspen trees grow in the high reaches. Elk, mule deer, raccoons, vultures, mountain lions, and black bears are a few of the animals that make their homes in the mountains.

As one drops back to the foothills and plains surrounding the mountains, the land begins to turn dry. Desert plants replace the green trees and abundant *vegetation*.

The insides of the mountains are riddled with limestone caves. Countless *fossils* have been found in this region, but visitors are asked to leave them where they are. *Geologists* come from all over the world to study these ancient rocks. The fossils are important links to help scientists understand how the Guadalupes began.

Scorpions live in the desert area above the Carlsbad Caverns.

ANIMALS OF THE AREA

Of all the animals, birds, and insects in the Carlsbad Caverns area, bats are the biggest attraction. But there are many other interesting creatures to study.

Inside the caverns live the cave crickets. These insects walk upside down on the ceilings and crawl along the floors and walls.

Outside the caverns live animals that have learned to adapt to the hot desert. Most of them sleep during the day and go out at night to feed. This way they can avoid the sun. Some small desert animals do not even need to drink water because they get the moisture they need from their diet of seeds.

The desert is a good place for snakes. Snakes are cold-blooded. That means they don't have to spend any of their energy either keeping warm or getting cool. Instead, their bodies adjust to whatever the air temperature is. Rattlesnakes store their rattles at the ends of their tails. When anyone comes too close, they shake their rattles as a warning to stay away.

Lizards are desert-lovers. A lizard can sit motionless for a long, long time.

When an insect flies by, the lizard lashes out with its long tongue. Before you can wiggle a finger, the insect has been eaten.

Scorpions sting like a bee or wasp. A scorpion's young are carried on its back—very handy for baby-sitting. In a few days, the babies are ready to go off on their own.

Mule deer live in many of the national parks. In Carlsbad Caverns National Park they roam from desert to mountain. They are named for their mule-like ears that can pick up danger sounds from far away. Their dull coloring helps them blend into rocks or sand, protecting them from mountain lions and other enemies.

The ringtail is a member of the raccoon family. It gets its name because of the rings on its tail. The ringtail likes mice and often goes into caves to hunt them out. It eats fruits and plants, too.

The gold-mantled ground squirrel looks like a chipmunk. It feeds on nuts and berries, and stuffs its cheeks just like the chipmunk. This animal whisks about, keeping up a busy chatter while hunting for food. When frightened, the squirrel gives a shrill cry, and runs and hides.

There are more than 300 kinds of birds in this region. The cactus wren is one. It builds a nest in a large cactus plant. The sharp spines protect both the bird and its eggs from snakes. Most of the cactus wren's diet is insects. From these insects it gets all the water it needs. When the cactus blooms in the spring, insects come right to the wren's door to get nectar from the flowers. The wren might catch dinner without even leaving its nest!

The roadrunner is a bird always on the move. It races along the side of the road and can go 15 or 20 miles an hour. If it wants to brake suddenly, it throws its long tail up to help it stop. The roadrunner eats insects, spiders, lizards, and young rattlesnakes.

Kangaroo rats also live in the desert. They are hard to catch, so most animals don't bother with them. Coyotes, though, have more patience than most animals. They will wait quietly for a long time outside the small animal's burrow. Their reward is kangaroo rat for dinner.

The speedy roadrunner pauses breifly before continuing its travels through the desert.

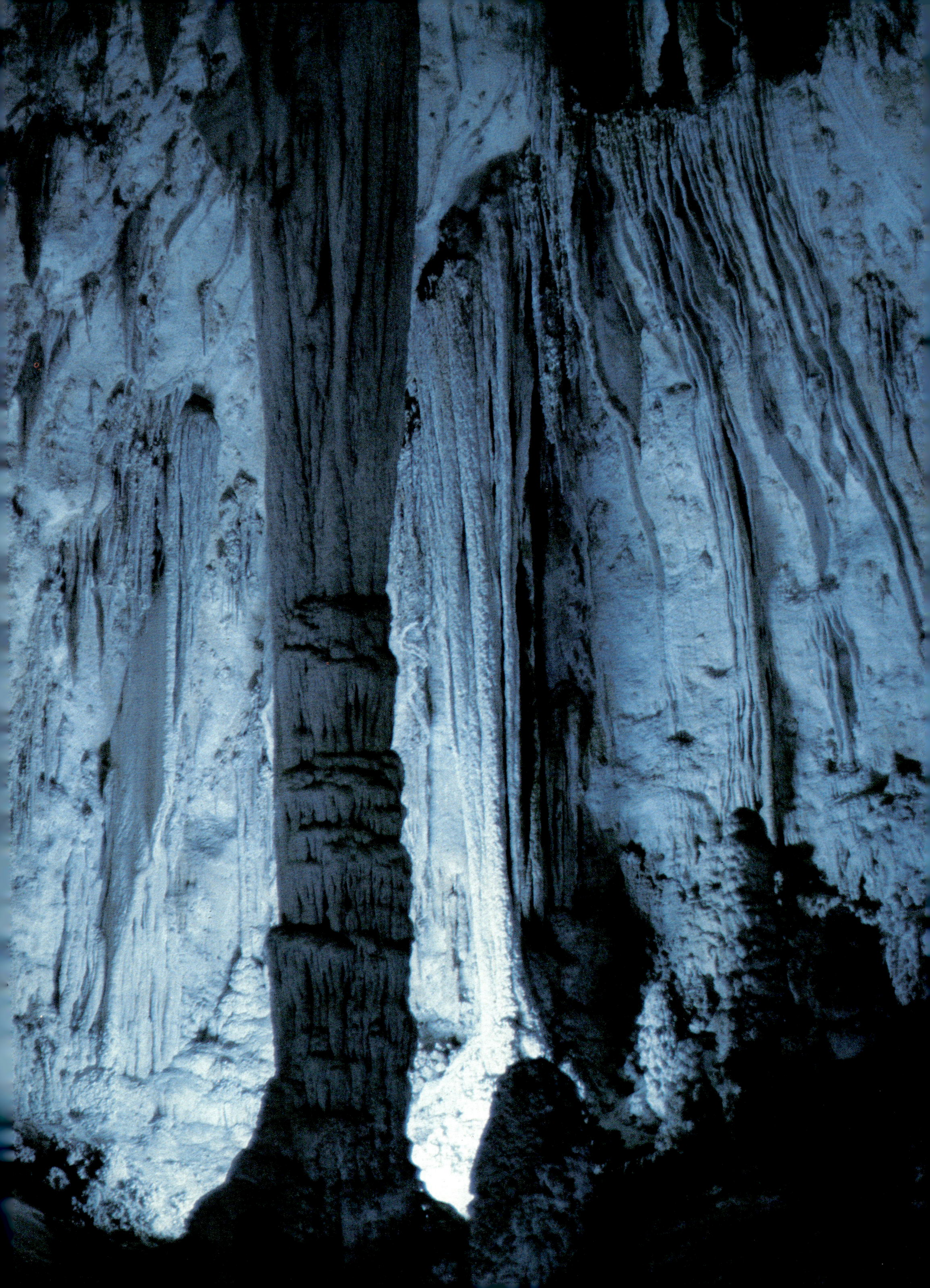

NEW CAVE

A *spelunker* is a person who explores caves. Those who want to be spelunkers and explore a cave without electric lights, paved paths, or modern restrooms will enjoy New Cave. This is 23 miles from the caverns. Visitors park in the lot at Slaughter Canyon, then hike a steep half-mile trail up to the cave entrance. A person needs to be in good physical condition to explore this place.

New Cave is really an old cave that was discovered in 1937 but is quite new to tourists. One must make a reservation to hike in New Cave. The rangers give tours every day during the summer and on weekends the rest of the year. Hikers are charged a fee. It is important to wear good walking shoes and take along a flashlight and water to drink.

Some years ago there was bat guano mining in this cave. There was also a time when vandals broke many of the beautiful formations, so now the cave is protected by gates.

The tour is one and one-fourth miles long. As the ranger lights the way with a lantern, fascinating sights show up in this wild cave. One formation is called Monarch. It is 89 feet high, and is believed to be the world's tallest column.

Christmas Tree is a very big, tan-colored stalagmite. It wears a mantle of white flowstone that looks like snow. Tiny flecks of crystal glitter like diamonds.

China Wall is another wonder. This ankle-high dam twists and turns for more than a mile. It is a tiny version of the Great Wall built long ago along the border of China.

The most famous formation in New Cave is a monster called The Klansman. He looks like a creature that has risen up from the underworld. His face is twisted and beast-like. He looks as if he has two rows of yellowish teeth. Tiny stalactites hang from his lips and make the wide mouth look as if Klansman is drooling. White flowstone covers his head and body. It looks like he's wearing a hooded fringed robe.

Tall columns of solid hardened minerals can reach a height of 89 feet.

EARLY PEOPLE OF THE REGION

Long before Jim White happened upon the caves, Native Americans roamed near the Carlsbad Caverns. The Basket Maker tribe are believed to have used the mouth of the cave as long as 2,000 years ago.

The cave entrance gave these early people protection from their enemies and the sudden storms that swept the desert. The entrance could hold as many as 100 people. Here they cooked and slept while they hid from other tribes or waited out a storm. On the entrance walls are the drawings they left, called *pictographs*. Most of the pictures are of plants. This probably means that these people depended on plants a great deal.

The first explorers of the caverns found a Basket Maker's sandal. Why only one? No one knows. Perhaps the person was lost. Or his torch may have gone out. Maybe he was frightened by something and left in a hurry.

Other Native Americans who lived in this area were the Mescalero people. *Mescal pits* ("cooking" pits) and grinding holes can still be seen near the caverns. Flint chips, broken arrow points, and bits of scattered pottery have been found. An occasional human skeleton or skull has turned up in the caverns, or has been found buried in the guano pits.

The land area around the caverns was a good place for the Native Americans to stay. The desert was warm, so they didn't need much clothing. Many kinds of cactus plants furnished tasty food. Hidden springs and pot holes provided water. Wood was scarce, but dry cactus plants, bushes, and plant stems fed the cooking fires.

An important desert food for the Native Americans was agave, which is also called century plant or *mescal*. This is where the name mescal pit comes from. Part of the mescal plant had clusters of leaves as big as cabbages.

To cook the mescal, the Native Americans dug large pits and lined them with flat rocks. Layers of mescal, wet grass, and earth were placed in the pits. Fires at both the top and bottom of the pit cooked the food. Large amounts of mescal might take several days to cook. Then it could be eaten or dried and stored. It was a healthy food and tasted a little like squash.

In the nearby canyons of the Guadalupe Mountains, nuts, berries, and seeds were added to the Native Americans' diet. Sparkling streams provided

FUN FACT The Basket Maker tribe was renamed The Pueblo tribe in the 1800s. They settled in southwestern United States. Their homes, made from sun-baked bricks, were built on high mesas. Mesas are flat-topped hills or cliffs with steep sides that protected the people from their enemies.

water, and wild animals furnished meat, skins, furs, and feathers.

Throughout the desert, plains, and mountain areas, there was a great abundance of game: buffalo, deer, wild turkeys, mountain sheep, antelopes, bears, rabbits, squirrels, quail, and other animals.

TAKING CARE IN THE PARK

Today, people who visit Carlsbad Caverns and the surrounding area must be careful. If you follow the rules while visiting Carlsbad Caverns National Park, you can be quite safe.

It is important to wear good hiking boots or rubber-soled shoes that don't

Agave was an important desert food for the early people who settled in the Carlsbad area.

slip easily. You'll also be more comfortable.

Before there were trails and electric lights in the caverns, there was the danger of getting lost. Jim White used to follow a long cord when he went into the caverns so he could find his way out again. Those who wander off the trails today still run the risk of getting lost or of slipping and falling. Always stay with an adult and on the trails.

There is also danger to the formations themselves. If people touch them, they may break. Fantastic shapes that have taken thousands of years to be created may be destroyed by one careless touch.

Outside the caverns, sudden changes in the weather can present danger. If thunderstorms with lightning or high winds come up suddenly, hikers must find shelter. Heavy rainstorms may cause flash floods in the canyons. Cliff climbing is also dangerous because the rock in the Guadalupe Mountains crumbles easily.

Poisonous snakes, desert centipedes, and scorpions must be avoided. Cactus plants won't bite or sting, but many of them have sharp spines that can tear your skin or clothes. Always stay on the marked trails and never hike alone.

Hiking on steep hills and mountain paths is not a good idea for a person with a weak heart or with a tendency to become dizzy.

Hypothermia is another danger. This happens when chilly weather and dampness cool one's body too much. The body can't get warm again and must have immediate medical treatment.

ACCOMMODATIONS IN THE CAVERNS

The trails in the caverns are carefully planned for people today. There are two tours to choose from. One is called the Blue Tour. This is a three-mile hike on which all the chambers open to the public can be seen. This tour takes between two and three hours. It is for those who have healthy hearts and no walking or breathing problems.

To begin this tour you must first hike down the steep trail to the caverns' entrance. You enter the cave and explore another steep, twisting trail through

FUN FACT New Cave was discovered by a goatherd named Tom Tucker while he was searching for his lost goats.

the Main Corridor and on through the Scenic Rooms. After climbing Appetite Hill, those who wish may eat in the underground lunchroom. From here the Blue Tour goes through Big Room.

The Red Tour begins at the visitor center above the caverns. It takes tourists by elevator straight down to Big Room where those in wheelchairs can wheel along with hikers and explore the formations in this huge room. This tour takes an hour and a half.

The caverns are open every day of the year except Christmas Day. Hours vary during the year so people should read the schedule posted at the visitor center. People can stroll or wheel at their own paces. Some tourists like to look at things a long time. Others prefer to move along faster, and not take

Hundreds of stalactites glitter like chandeliers in King's Palace.

in all the details. Rangers are on hand to answer questions and give information. At certain times the rangers give guided tours.

The caverns stay at 56°F all year so a light jacket or sweater feels good. The temperatures outside average 90°F in summer and between 50°F and 60°F in winter.

AREA INFORMATION

There are no campgrounds, hotels, or motels within Carlsbad Caverns National Park. Neither private camping nor campfires are allowed. However, there are two cities close to the caverns that have facilities.

The city of Carlsbad is 20 miles from the caverns. The Guadalupe Mountains foothills are on one side of the city and desert plains on the other. Carlsbad has many motels and several campgrounds.

The city of Carlsbad also has a special attraction called Living Desert. This is a state park with plants and animals from the Chihuahuan Desert. Visitors walk along trails to see 60 species of desert birds, mammals, and reptiles. There are also thousands of desert plants on display along the trails and in the greenhouse.

White's City is seven miles from the caverns near the mouth of Walnut Canyon. This area was homesteaded in 1927 by a man named Charlie White. (Charlie White was a friend of Jim White, but the two were not related). White built a camp for tourists who wanted to see the caverns. Later the place was named White's City in his honor.

At White's City there is a campground, motel, and other facilities. Buses leave for the caverns four times a day.

ACTIVITIES ABOVE GROUND

There are many things to see and do above ground at Carlsbad Caverns National Park. Here are a few ideas:

Walnut Canyon Loop Drive is a nine-and-one-half mile drive you can take on a gravel road. The trip takes about 45 minutes and shows off desert canyon country.

You can begin a half-mile desert nature walk at the Carlsbad visitor center.

FUN FACT More than 20 miles of the Carlsbad Caverns have been explored, but only a few miles are open to the public. Cave specialists are discovering new rooms and passageways all the time.

Look at desert plants and flowers that have been labeled with their names.

Some people like hiking adventures above ground as well as below. At Carlsbad Caverns National Park there are old ranch trails to follow. Because these trails are not marked, you should first get advice and a map from a ranger.

Whether you hike above ground or explore the formations, Carlsbad Caverns National Park is full of adventures!

Visitors can gather at one of the entrances to Carlsbad to safely watch the bats leave for their nightly hunt.

FOR MORE PARK INFORMATION

For more information about Carlsbad Caverns, write to:

Carlsbad Caverns National Park Visitor Center
3225 National Parks Highway
Carlsbad, NM 88220

PARK MAP

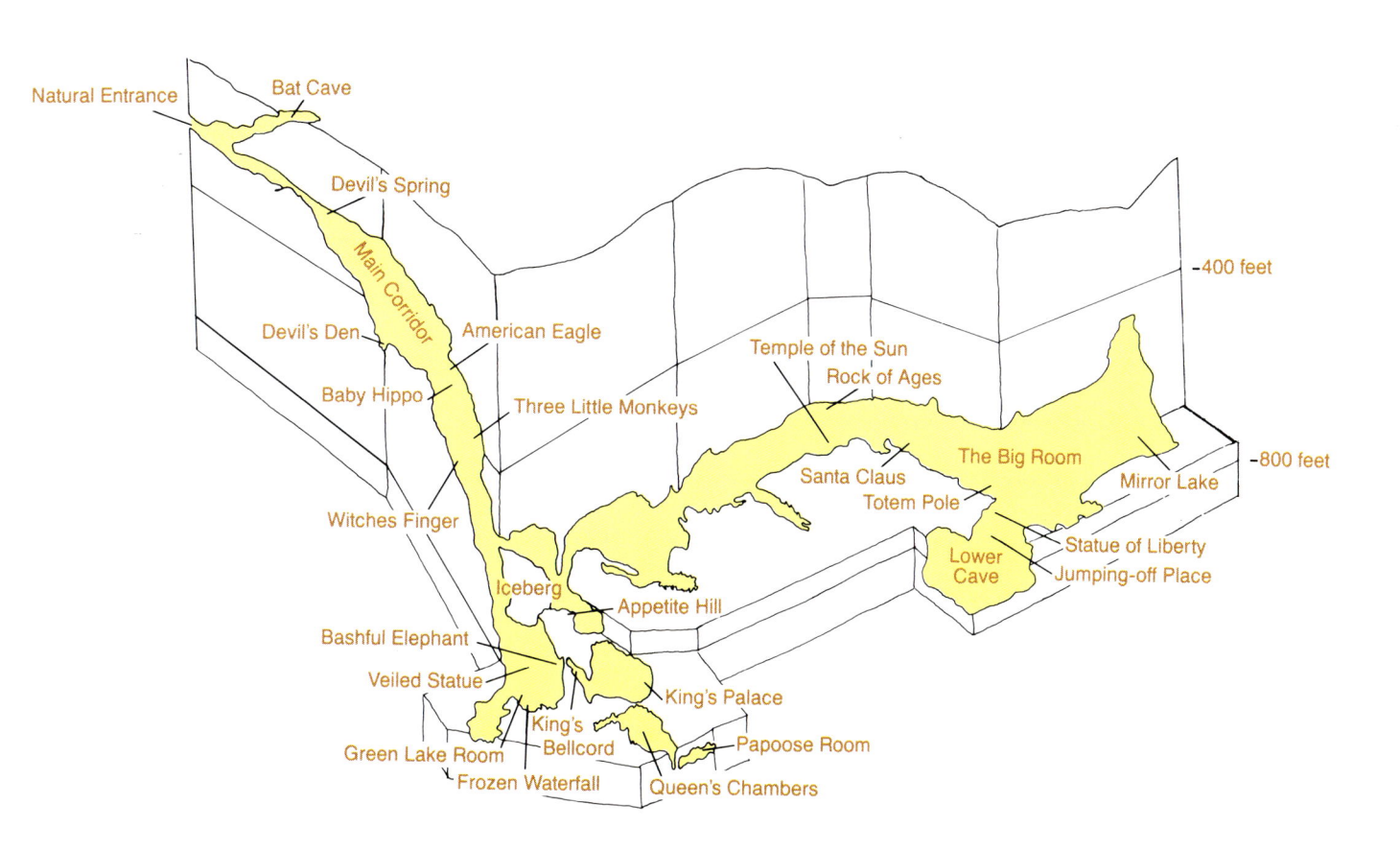

Carlsbad Caverns National Park

45

GLOSSARY/INDEX

ALGAE *17*—A colony of tiny plants usually found in water or damp places like caves.

BAT GUANO *26, 27, 37, 38*— Bat droppings.

CARBONIC ACID *17*—A weak acid that slowly destroyed the limestone rocks found in the Carlsbad area, helping create the caverns.

CAVE PEARLS *9*—Mineral coatings that grew on grains of sand to make round, glistening balls.

FLOWSTONE *9, 12, 13, 37*— Colorful mineral coverings on the floors and walls of caves.

FOSSIL *33*—The print of a plant or animal body that has hardened into rock.

GEOLOGIST *33*—A person who studies the history of the earth and how its changes are recorded in rocks and rock formations.

HELICTITES *9*— Mineral formations with many crystal branches, resembling bushes and other plants.

HYPOTHERMIA *40*—A condition where the body cools to a dangerous, life-threatening level.

KEROSENE *5, 7*—An oil burned in lanterns for light and also used to run heaters.

LILY PADS *9*—Minerals that have formed on top of cavern pools and look like lily pads.

LIMESTONE *17, 20*—A rock formed over thousands of years by the settling and build-up of animals and plants.

MESCAL *38*—A desert plant.

MESCAL PITS *38*—Cooking pits.

PICTOGRAPHS *38*—Pictures painted on rocks by prehistoric people.

SONOR SYSTEM *24*—A way of locating objects by bouncing sound waves off them; bats use sonar to find food and avoid obstacles.

SPELUNKER *37*—A person who explores caves.

STALACTITES *7, 9, 11, 12, 13, 14, 15, 17, 21, 37*—Mineral formations that "grow" from the ceiling of a cave when water drips, leaving behind a mineral deposit.

STALAGMITES *9, 11, 14, 15, 21, 37*—Mineral formations that "grow" up from the floor of a cave when evaporated water drops leave behind a mineral deposit.
SWITCHBACK *7*—A road or path that zigzags back and forth.
VEGETATION *33*—Plants, bushes, and trees.